HOW TO TALK GOLF

David Langdon's

A–Z of Golfing Terms

D1523628

Eyre Methuen · London

Some books by the same author

HOME FRONT LINES
ALL BUTTONED UP
LANGDON AT LARGE
PUNCH WITH WINGS
HOW TO PLAY GOLF AND STAY HAPPY
DAVID LANGDON'S CASEBOOK

First published in 1975
Copyright © David Langdon
Printed in Great Britain for
Eyre Methuen Ltd
11 New Fetter Lane, London EC4P 4EE
by Cox & Wyman Ltd
Fakenham, Norfolk

ISBN 0 413 34250 6

FOREWORD

It is statute and ordained that in na place of the Realme
there be used Fute-ball, Golfe, or other sik unproffitable
sportis, (being against) the common good of the Realme
and defense thereof.

James I V of Scotland, 1491

The terminology of golf is strictly, if not always clearly,
defined in the Rules of Golf as formulated by the Royal
and Ancient Golf Club of St Andrews, the governing
body of the game. Golf may be played by a newcomer
with only a tenuous knowledge of the Rules, and in time
he will learn the more important rudiments from others
better versed in them. There is never a lack of such people
in any club eager to point the error of another member's
ways. By then, however, he will also have picked up a
whole new *patois* of expressions which embroider the
language of golf, as with any living language, and which
are common currency wherever the game is played.

I think this volume is the first attempt to include in the
form of a glossary both the standard terminology and the
jargon of the game. I hope it will serve as a quick and
handy reference book for the average club player so that
he will be able to talk golf at the Nineteenth with the best
of them. I hope too it will be of service to the golf widow,
enabling her to converse intelligently with her husband
on the rare occasions when they do meet. It may also
be useful to lay readers, helping them to follow the
proliferation of golf tournaments on their tellies with a
better understanding.

3

Golf theologians, that small but admirable junta of geriatrics who commandeer a corner of every clubhouse bar, will no doubt be outraged by the infelicities and inaccuracies in any work on golf which does not aspire to be one of scholarship. To them I make no apologies, as they thrive on and enjoy arguing the minutiae of a game which owes more to art than to science.

I am indebted to Mr S. Walter Butterworth, a fellow club member and a true *aficionado*, for his helpful comments during the preparation of the manuscript.

DL

Ritual of the address

Address   A term made familiar to the non-golfing public by the music hall comedian Sid Field, who addressed the ball verbally in his famous golfing sketch – 'Dear ball'. A player has 'addressed the ball' when he has taken his stance and grounded his club. In HAZARDS, however, where the club may not be grounded prior to making a STROKE, a player has 'addressed the ball' when he has merely taken his stance. There are as many individual styles of settling down to a stance, waggling the club-head and generally preparing for the backswing, as there are players. Anyone nearby making the slightest move-ment or noise during the Ritual of the Address merits a withering look, and apologies for such behaviour are among the most abject in golf.

Advice   A player in a competition may not seek or give advice except from or to his partner or his caddie or his partner's caddie. Giving advice, even if it is not sought, incurs a swingeing PENALTY of two strokes. The agon-ized appeal of 'What the *hell* am I doing?' made by a player having a poor round should in charity be regarded as purely rhetorical and not as an official request for advice. One of the advantages of using a golf-trolley instead of a caddie is that it can't confuse you with advice.

5

'What do you suggest here?'

'Agricultural' Description of a poor shot in which the ball is struck a violent blow, the club-head taking a larger DIVOT than is necessary.

Air shot A STROKE made when a ball is aimed at with the club but completely missed, thereby counting as a stroke, unless you can contrive to make it look like a mere practice swing.

Agricultural

Albatross A hole completed in three STROKES under the PAR for that hole. A rare bird.

Amateur As distinct from a professional golfer. One who plays golf solely as a non-remunerative or non-profit sport, e.g. the ordinary club golfer. As in other sports, a definition beset with problems. Club golfers who continually win golf balls as wagers by playing off false HANDICAPS are considered to be border-line cases.

'Am I in your way?' A question asked on the green by a player whose ball appears to be in line with another player's putt (*see* STYMIE, now archaic). If affirmed, the player lifts his ball, marks its position and replaces it after the other player's putt is taken. A useful ploy (The Langdon Gambit) is to put the question when your ball is geometrically nowhere near your opponent's line of putt. Addressing his ball, his mind will be focusing on the absurdity of your suggestion rather than on the putt, and the result could well be a foozled shot.

'Angel raper' Over-stated description of a drive lofted unnecessarily skywards.

Lofted skywards

Annual dinner   A Golf Club annual function, usually stag. Barely tolerable unless you are fully pre-primed with liquid refreshment. Avoid like the plague being invited to another Club's annual dinner, unless you enjoy endless and often inarticulate speeches larded with in-jokes and other incomprehensible allusions.

Appointment   A date made for a game of golf. To be late for any reason short of sudden death (and this only your own demise) is regarded as an appalling social gaffe by golfers who will stand you up on any date unconnected with golf and think nothing of it. The sacrosanct and contractual nature of a golf appointment is impossible to explain to wives who manage, often with subconscious motivation, to arrange last-minute errands ensuring that their golfer husbands will miss their appointments on the first tee.

Golf appointment . . .

Approach   Any SHOT from fairway to green, the distance depending on your standard of play. The good player always aims to put the ball within easy putting distance of the PIN. The mediocre player is blissfully content if the ball lands anywhere on the green at all from an approach shot.

Apron   The perimeter or cut area around a green. A favourite outer ring for the RABBIT when he is aiming to be PIN-HIGH.

Artisan or **'artesian'** (corrupt.)   A workingman golfer whose membership fee is nominal, but whose times of starting on the course seem to be restricted to the hours just before dusk or just after dawn. Often SCRATCH players of breathtaking modesty. With the blurring of pay differentials these days, most artisan golfers, especially skilled workers, are in a higher income bracket than the average full member. A candidate for membership of the artisan section is usually vetted in the first place by an Artisan's Committee who decide if he is 'one of them', a refreshing case of class distinction in reverse.

Assistance   In making a STROKE a player shall not accept or seek physical assistance (*see* 'LEATHER MASHIE') or protection from the elements. Thus in wet weather a caddie may not hold an umbrella over a player, but the player is permitted to hold an umbrella over himself with one hand and make a stroke with the other. An example of a dispensation not noted for its generosity.

Assistant   A polite and engaging young man, beautifully attired, who assists the professional in running the pro's shop and giving lessons. Quietly ambitious, he is a bird of passage, always rushing off to take on a full pro's job at a small country course or living it up somewhere remote and exotic, e.g. the Country Club at Gezira or Addis Ababa.

'Attacking shot' A charitable term applied to your opponent's putt when he is in a losing position and sends his ball whistling irretrievably past the hole.

Attend The act of holding the flagstick in the hole at the request of your opponent or partner, prior to his taking his putt, ready to remove the stick if the ball looks like being sunk. A pedantic opponent may leave the stick in the hole and claim that the request 'Attend, please' was not made clearly and audibly in advance.

Away, awa' You are said to be 'Away' when your ball is farther from the hole than your opponent's, so that it is your turn to play. Ben Hogan during one of his less laconic rounds said 'You are away' to his opponent on all of the eighteen greens. Another useful gambit – always use the Scottish vernacular where available. 'You're awa'' gives your opponent the impression that you have some ancestral connection with the homeland of golf and hence some added native expertise. (*See also* 'NAE BOTHER'.)

Backspin   A motion imparted to a ball by an expert, causing the club-head to come into contact with it when moving in a downward direction, arresting the ball's run on the green towards the hole. More effective than any amount of shouting 'Whoa!', 'Stop, you blighter!' or 'Sit!'

Baffy   Old fashioned term for a No. 3 wood.

Ball   The white dimpled spheroid, now rubber or plastic-cored, which has replaced the old 'guttie' or gutta-percha ball of yesteryear and the older 'feather' ball. The British or 'small' ball measures 1·62″ in diameter and weighs 1·62 ounces. The American or 'larger' ball is 0·06″ bigger in diameter but weighs the same. In spite of long controversy, both sizes of ball are still in use, although the Royal and Ancient has now made the use of the larger ball compulsory in all OPEN tournaments. Advocates of the larger ball as being easier to hit ignore the simple arithmetic of comparing the circumference of the ball with that of Mother Earth. The average golfer will take little convincing that the chances of hitting the ball rather than the ground aren't all that improved by a margin of 0·06″.

0·06" margin

'Ball-a-ball-a-ball'   The normal wager in Club games is one ball on the MATCH. ('A ball of the finest quality, in its original wrapper, in mint condition.') Inveterate gamblers, however, stake three balls on the outcome of a match, one ball on the first half, one on the second and a third on the result of the whole match. More cautious players can be shamed into such profligacy after a liquid lunch. (*See* 'NASSAU'.)

Beginner's loop (or slice)   A shot that starts off in a straight trajectory but then fades inexorably to the right (or left, in the case of a left-handed player). All too familiar to the beginner and the average golfer. If perpetrated by a class golfer it is described by him brazenly as a 'controlled fade'. Many other synonyms and a host of suggested remedies but no permanent cure.

Birdie   A hole completed in one STROKE under PAR or BOGEY. In this connection see ALBATROSS, EAGLE, drawn from a more exotic ornithology. Whereas with birdie the common or garden kind must serve for the lesser performance.

Bisque A STROKE, or strokes, conceded in MATCH play, and taken when and where the receiver of the bisque decides, not necessarily at the holes where his HANDICAP stroke is normally taken. More than one bisque may be taken at a hole and there is no need for the player to announce his intention before the hole is played out, but only before leaving the green. One of the more friendly variations in the game of golf (*see* 'CLIENT'S GAME') but if anyone conceding bisques imagines that the receiver will forbear taking a bisque on a short PAR-three hole he will often be mistaken.

Blaster A sand iron or sand wedge, a weapon with an open face intended for extricating a bunkered ball and put to maximum use by the mediocre golfer.

Blind An approach position from which the green cannot be seen.

Bogey The PAR figure for a hole, or in aggregate, for the course. The score which a SCRATCH player might be expected to take. In America, however, 'bogey' is one *over* par, and a player who drops a STROKE at any hole is said to have 'bogeyed' it. Two over par to an American is a 'double-bogey'. So it's no use boasting to an American cousin of the number of bogeys you have made in a round. The term 'bogey' was introduced in 1891, and is said to derive from a mythical Colonel Bogey whose game was described as 'uniformly steady but never over brilliant'.

Bore Every Golf Club can produce a short list of bores, but only one may qualify as *The* Club Bore, and he would be the one least aware of his status. Anyone can merit inclusion in a short list by habitually giving a shot-by-shot account of his last round of golf in the NINETEENTH.

Borrow A mysterious quality which you can, according to most caddies, impart to a ball on a green, to take account of any surface contours. A putt directed by him and which goes wildly left or right of the hole is said by him to have been given too much or too little borrow. A putt which you sink by ignoring his advice is still claimed by him as being due to his advice.

Brassie   A No. 2 wood.

Bunker   Sand-trap (USA). A man-made pit dug in fairways and in front of greens, filled with sand, flints, footprints and other objects, and diabolically placed to engulf shots made to the green by lesser players. No loose impediments may be removed before playing out of a bunker, not even old banana skins, which, according to a recent decision of the Royal and Ancient, are 'natural objects' and therefore loose impediments.

Bye   The hole or holes remaining after a MATCH has been decided, and played as a new game, generally for

Club bore

the purpose of an additional or minor wager, the excuse being to keep interest in the rest of the game alive, but really in the hope that the loser up to that point can recoup a little of what he has already lost, or the winner add to what he has already won.

Bye-bye The hole or holes remaining after a bye has been decided and played as a new game.

Caddie, caddy Der. *Cadet* (Fr.) or 'little chief'. A term applied in Edinburgh in the eighteenth century to young loafers. Uppity caddies can usefully be reminded of this derivation. The archetypal Club caddie, cloth-capped, muffled against all weathers, is a fast disappearing breed in the affluent society. He is being replaced by the mechanical trolley and in school holidays by youngsters seeking pin money. The old caddie was often a know-ledgeable character, a good ball-finder (if not yours, some-one else's), a bit of a martinet, always hinting that he once played off SCRATCH, safe in the knowledge that he would never be challenged to prove it. Elderly Club members with nostalgia clouded by the passage of time regret their passing, and refer to the younger caddies (if indeed they can be found) as mere 'trolley-pushers' or 'bag-carriers'. (*See* 'STRAIGHT AT THE BACK OF THE 'OLE, SIR'.)

Call through The act of calling a MATCH following you to overtake. A mark of etiquette but rare other than in dire emergency, e.g. a lost ball. (*See* 'COME THROUGH WHEN YOU LIKE'.)

'Mr Captain, sir *!'*

Captain An annual appointee, selected by the Club Committee by democratic vote or by a caucus decision. Usually the previous vice-captain. Apart from leading the Club team into battle in inter-club or county matches, a captain's function is largely a social one and involves a degree of financial solvency on his part. He is an *ex-officio* member of committees, gives cocktail parties, presides over the annual Captain's Day Competition and generally tries to make himself affable around the Clubhouse. In return he has the honour of 'driving himself into the job', actually hitting off ceremonially from the first tee with a brand new ball which is retrieved by a senior caddie as a perk, to cheers and catcalls from assembled members straight from the NINETEENTH. He also takes precedence of play on the course over all other members. He should command respect to the extent of the mock obsequies of doffing one's cap or touching the forelock and murmuring 'Mr Captain, *sir*', in his presence. The more ambitious member, sweating on a vice-captaincy, will employ other servilities, such as plying the captain with drinks at the bar and with invitations to dinner. During any captain's year of office there is always a disgruntled faction of members who will decry the current incumbent's best efforts and suggest other members who would have made a 'good captain', often in a transparent attempt to mask their own disappointment at being passed over.

Card Score card. A folded oblong sheet available in the Clubhouse or pro shop on which is printed the yardage, PAR and STROKE index of each hole on the course, with spaces for the marker's and player's score and for the result of each hole. You do not mark your own card for obvious reasons. The score card is intended for recording a player's score primarily in competitions, but is torn up by the thousand in disgust or despair with never a thought for the cost of all that lovely printing. (*See* 'WHENEVER I GET A CARD IN MY HAND'.)

Carry The distance from the point at which a ball is hit to where it first strikes the ground.

Casual water Any temporary accumulation of water visible, according to the Rules, 'before or after' a player takes his stance. Snow and ice are included. A ball in casual water may be retrieved and dropped without PENALTY but not nearer the hole. If in casual water in a HAZARD it may be picked up and dropped either in the dry part of the hazard or behind it for one penalty stroke. This Rule bravely deals with freak weather conditions which would send the average golfer scuttling back to the shelter of the Clubhouse.

Chip   An elevated approach SHOT to the green intended to PITCH and run to the flag but often landing in the yawning bunkers surrounding the green. The 'Chipper', an open-faced iron with a broad sole, was introduced by club makers specially for this shot, and golfers having trouble with their chip shots rushed out to buy chippers by the thousand, but as with most innovations it was just another case of 'workman blaming tool' when satisfaction was not achieved.

Choke down (USA)   To close the face of a club or grip a club lower down the shaft, for specialized shots. Best left to the expert.

Chole (Fr.)   A fifteenth-century game half-way between hockey and golf and said to be the forerunner of golf. May account for the curious strokes reminiscent of other games still evident in the game of golf.

Cleek (Archaic Scot.)   An iron club. 'Hand me m'cleek' can be relied on to unnerve an opponent.

'Client's game'   A friendly invitation MATCH between a member and a business associate in which such ingratiating devices as BISQUES and MULLIGANS and conceding of putts by the member are liberally employed.

'Come on heat'   A player who suddenly contrives to produce a single good SHOT amid a welter of indifferent ones is said by his opponent to have 'come on heat'.

'Come through when you like'   An open invitation by one MATCH to a match following to overtake them at an early opportunity. Usually a tongue-in-cheek offer which should be understood as 'Come through if you *can*.' (cf. CALL THROUGH.)

'Commercial'   A SHOT devoid of elegance in execution but effective in its result. (*See also* 'NOT HOW, BUT HOW MANY'.)

Committee A group, caucus or clique often self-appointed and self-perpetuating to take charge of greens, social events, kitchen, HANDICAPS or finance at your Club.

Committeeman A chap who is quite normal and friendly but once appointed to a committee suddenly turns all toffee-nosed and nasty when you complain about the greens or the food.

Toffee-nosed

Competition   A golf MATCH officially organized by the Club Committee in which players go off in SINGLES or FOURSOMES at specified times. Apart from regular monthly competitions (MEDAL, STABLEFORD), there are running competitions on a knock-out basis extending over a seasonal period, and special competitions for cups and other trophies, often named in memory of members long since elevated to honorary membership of Elysium G C. By tradition, money prizes won in competitions are translated by the winners into free drinks all round at the bar.

Concede   The act of giving up a putt or a hole to your opponent. There is an implication of grace here but in fact many players only concede where there is no alternative. Conceding putts in MATCH play can involve a degree of gamesmanship. If your short putts are giving you trouble, it is policy to concede any fairly long putt with which your opponent is faced at an early stage in the match. This will surprise him for its generosity, but from that point on he may be shamed into conceding the short putts with which you are having difficulty. Or, of course, he may not, but it is worth the gamble.

Cotton, Henry   A British golf ace. Ended long run of American victories in the OPEN in 1934 with an historic round of 65, the Dunlop 65 ball being named in his honour for this performance. An entire supply of cotton shirts was once sold to some Japanese visitors at Henry's pro shop at Temple G C because they thought the shirts were named after him.

Cup   1. A trophy or 'pot' won in a golf competition, usually held for a year. Handed over by the previous winner often with the unconvincing remark that he's relieved at not having to keep it polished for another year. 2. The actual hole sunk in the green holding the flagstick. 3. Something filled to the brim with bitterness. Or not, as the case may be. It depends on your day's play.

Dead, lie A ball is said to 'lie dead' when it is so near the hole that sinking the putt is a 'dead' certainty. (*But see* 'NOBBUT A MINUTE'.)

Default Conceding a MATCH to an opponent without playing against him; to fail to appear for a scheduled match. (*See* APPOINTMENT.)

Discontinuance of play In MEDAL play a game may not be discontinued on account of bad weather or for any reason other than danger from lightning or sudden illness. Sticklers for RULES can get themselves soaking wet in foul weather waiting on slow players ahead and declining to take shelter. You may not endear yourself to them by taking shelter, pleading an imaginary flash of lightning, but at least you will keep dry.

Distance The linear measure between the spot from which a ball is struck badly and that at which it is assumed lost. A second ball can be dropped at this spot and struck again, incurring two PENALTY shots for 'Stroke and Distance'. It takes rare strength of character in such a situation to accept the double penalty resignedly without

asking for the RULE to be checked in case only one penalty SHOT is involved.

Divot   A sliver of turf dug up (or 'taken') by striking at a ball, normally with an iron club. A well-struck iron SHOT should involve the 'taking' of a divot (but cf. 'AGRICULTURAL'). Divots should be replaced and stamped down before proceeding to the next shot, especially if within sight of a committeeman or the greenkeeper or a member of his staff.

Silent umbrage

'Do please carry on' A plea lacking in sincerity made by a player who has struck his ball into deep rough, to those helping him search for it, after a decent interval. Silent umbrage, however, is taken by the player if his helpers actually take him up on his offer and walk off leaving him to look for his ball on his own.

Dog-leg A fairway which takes a sharp left or right turn in the shape of a dog's hind leg towards the green, so that the flagstick is unsighted from the tee. A polite host should warn his guest of the topography of a dog-leg hole *before* the latter takes his drive.

'Don't want that one back' A predictable and boring remark (cf. 'ONE!', 'SHOT!') made to a player when he has hit a good shot from the tee. It is suggested that the Royal and Ancient be approached to consider framing a RULE inflicting one or more PENALTY STROKES on any player making such a remark.

Dormie State of the game when a player or his side is as many holes UP as there are remaining to play. Said to derive from Latin *dormire* 'to sleep'; the player who is 'dormie' cannot lose even if he falls asleep. But strictly he would have to keep going to the last green and score at least a HALF on one of the remaining holes to win the match.

Double-bogey (USA) *See* BOGEY, and add one.

Double-figure A golfer with a handicap from ten to twenty-four. (*See* SINGLE-FIGURE.)

Down In MATCH play, a side is 'down' when it has lost more holes than it has won. (cf. UP.)

Draw A miracle SHOT which starts off looking like a HOOK and suddenly corrects itself in mid-air. If performed by anyone other than a class player it would be as well to examine the ball for a cut or other defect, as this may well be the cause of its erratic trajectory.

Drive The first SHOT from tee to fairway, or green in the case of short holes. The longest drive on record so far is 445 yards, a statistic best forgotten for fear of pressing with your own drives. (*See* 'ANGEL RAPER'.)

Dropping   The time-honoured principle of golf is that 'the ball be played as it lies'. Where, however, a ball is unplayable (e.g. deep in a water HAZARD, behind trees, on ground under repair) it may be lifted and dropped under the RULES. The player must stand erect, face the hole and drop the ball over his shoulder, as near as possible to the spot where the original ball lay, but not nearer the hole. You can often win a quick wager from players who insist on the *left* shoulder, as the Rules do not specify which shoulder.

Eagle The phenomenon of taking two STROKES less than BOGEY at a hole. Thus a hole-in-one on a PAR-three hole could technically be described as an eagle, but such pedantry would be lost on members in the rush to the bar.

Eclectic A competition under STROKE conditions where two or more rounds are played and the eclectic score is the best score of each hole in all the rounds. One of the more esoteric competitions in the game, containing a strong element of self-delusion.

'Effortless' Description by a friendly partner of one of your rare good shots into which you have poured every ounce of effort.

'Erratic' A generous description of the normal play of most mediocre golfers.

Etiquette, Rules of A set of nine rules, separate from the actual Rules of Golf, intended as a Code of Behaviour in Golf. No penalties incurred for breaches, other than outraged glances and feelings and the occasional sneaky letter of complaint to the secretary.

Rule 1. **No one should move, talk or stand close or directly behind the ball or the hole when a player is addressing the ball or making a stroke.** A breach of this rule may not always be due to ignorance. The judicious rattling of the contents of a golf bag, or the loose change in your pocket, at the top of your opponent's swing at a critical stage of the game can often win you the hole. Only a mean opponent will accept your offer to let him take the shot again. Similarly the device of standing behind a player taking his tee shot or behind the hole when he is taking his putt is practised by people long after their attention has been drawn to this infringement, as is the more subtle one of arranging your shadow to fall over your opponent's ball and waggling the shadow slightly as he makes his downswing.

Rule 2. **The player who has the 'HONOUR' should be allowed to play before his opponent or fellow-competitor tees the ball.** This rule can be tiresome at times because it shows at a glance to the group of players following behind which of you lost the last hole. If they are TIGERS whose progress your match has been delaying, it gives them a shrewd idea, but not always an accurate one, which of your own group is the weaker player and therefore at whom to direct their animosity.

Rule 3. **No player should play until the players in front are out of range.** 'Out of range' here means farther than your longest drive can possibly reach. One of the more curious paradoxes of the game shows itself when you take a chance on the rule and drive off with the assurance that you could not possibly reach the players ahead. With no apparent effort or conscious change of stance or swing, you invariably proceed to pull off the longest drive of your golfing career, your ball landing squarely in, if not actually on, the group of startled players 275 yards ahead. No amount of shouting 'FORE!' or 'So very sorry, I'd *no* idea I could ever reach you', will retrieve the situation.

Rule 4. **In the interest of all, players should play without delay.** Ken Bousfield has gone on record for playing 18 holes in 91 minutes, taking 68 strokes. Two and a half hours is a more usual time for a SINGLES, and three to four hours for a THREE- or FOURBALL MATCH. Japanese visitors, etiquette-conscious to a fault, have been known to take five hours to play a fourball. A match which has one clear hole ahead should allow the following match to overtake them. More acrimony and hard feelings are stirred up among members for slow play and 'holding up the course' than for any other infringement of the Rules of Etiquette.

Rule 5. **Players searching for a ball should allow other players coming up to pass them; they should signal to the players following them to pass, and should not continue their play until those players have passed and are out of range.** (*See* CALL THROUGH.) The mediocre player when called through in these circumstances is always liable not to produce his best effort, having been put on his mettle and with an added audience. His own drive may well find the rough, and in the ensuing embarrassing confusion it is very difficult for the match called through to insist on keeping its place. Some sort of compromise should be reached, however, and the situation unsnarled before a third match appears on the tee.

Rule 6. **Before leaving a bunker a player should carefully fill up all holes made by him therein.** The constant breach of this rule is evident to any lesser player who has regular occasion to play out of a bunker, unless it happens to be one just vacated by a greenkeeper with a rake. Being forced to play out of someone else's oversize footprints, which may not be smoothed down before play, sets up a chain reaction. You have to be a pretty altruistic type to smooth out the offending footprint as well as those you yourself have made. You can, however, put this to good account by loudly calling the attention of any player standing nearby to the disgraceful state of the bunker, and then ostentatiously set about smoothing the surface down, glowing with self-righteousness.

Rule 7. **Through the green, a player should ensure that any turf cut or displaced by him is replaced at once and pressed down, and that after players have**

Outsize footprint

holed out, any damage to the putting green made by the ball or player is carefully repaired. Replaced DIVOTS are often turned over by crows in search of whatever in the food line lies beneath a freshly divoted turf. A member of the greens committee who has spotted you ignoring a divot will, however, not be mollified by your blaming a crow cawing away in a neighbouring tree.

Rule 8. **Players should ensure that, when dropping bags or the flagstick, no damage is done to the putting green, and that neither they nor their caddies damage the hole by standing close to the hole or in handling the flagstick. The flagstick should be properly replaced in the hole before players leave the putting green.** This rule is clearly meant to discourage any display of temper on the greens, when a missed putt could lead to putters and flagsticks being thrown about in disgust, or to players dropping in their tracks sobbing hysterically and kicking up the turf with their heels in a tantrum. It has also been known for players to walk off the green with the flagstick stuck absent-mindedly in their golf bag, while they are immersed in writing up their score cards.

Rule 9. **When the play of a hole is completed, players should immediately leave the putting green.** Most long HANDICAP players will have wrung every ounce of interest out of a hole by the time they reach the green and are only too glad to see the back of it. Others find the green a useful resting place to hold post mortems on their play or to check their score cards. An ear-splitting yell of 'FORE!' will serve to break up such cosy groups.

Exerting influence The RULES stipulate that no player or caddie shall 'take any action to influence the position or movement of a ball'. Presumably this does not preclude the common practice of yelling encouragement to a ball to stop, stay out, sit or drop.

Immersed

Fade A class player's controlled SLICE but a false description of a beginner's slice. (*See also* BEGINNER'S LOOP.)

Fairway The cut area running from tee to green with 'semi' and long rough on both sides, fairly easily determined on a well-kept course. On long holes the object is the time-honoured one of 'keeping the ball on the fairway', and a player who has had the misfortune of a succession of shots into the rough may be excused the sad, rhetorical call to his partner or opponent 'What are the fairways like?'

'Fantastic!' Description of any good but flukey shot made by a RABBIT, usually by an opponent who stands rooted, arms akimbo, looking at you with insulting incredulity.

Fibrositis A type of muscular ailment regularly used as an excuse for bad golf.

Flagstick The RULES define a flagstick as 'a moveable straight indicator with or without bunting [*sic*] or other

Insulting incredulity

material attached, centred in the hole to show its position. It shall be circular in cross-section'. Generally, the flag-stick is of wood, metal or plastic, painted in black and white stripes, those in the 'out' holes (one to nine) fly a yellow flag (or bunting), those in the 'in' or 'home' holes (ten to eighteen) fly a red flag.

'Fluff'   A poorly executed shot, due to any one of a dozen reasons.

Follow through   The act of throwing the arms up and towards the hole after striking the ball. An essential element of the swing, as any pro will tell you *ad nauseam* during a golf lesson.

'Fore!'   Said to derive from ''Ware before!', i.e. those in front beware. A warning cry to indicate your ball is flying or about to fly near other players. Often shouted immediately *after* impact when some such explanation as light travelling faster than sound is rarely acceptable to the aggrieved party. Check now that your golf insurance premium is paid up, indeed, that you have one at all.

Fourball   A match between two sides of two players, each player playing his own ball, but in each pair the better of the two scores for each hole counts as the score of the partnership for that hole. In the USA this is usually called a FOURSOME, just to confuse matters.

Foursome   A match between two sides of two players, each side playing only one ball, the partners driving off at alternate tees and thereafter playing alternate shots on the way to the hole. In the USA and Canada this is usually called a 'Scotch Foursome', to distinguish it from a 'Foursome', which is the same as our FOURBALL. Get it?

Free drop   1. A ball can be lifted and dropped over the shoulder in certain situations without PENALTY. 2. What a caddie is sometimes handed in liquid form from the club bar by a member for whom he has caddied and who has had a good round of golf.

'Friendly'   A match played on a friendly basis (i.e. not under MEDAL conditions) in which putts may be conceded and RULES slightly bent by mutual consent. Such matches often turn out to bely the description.

Gallery Any number of spectators from one to a thousand, or more. A bunch of people sipping highballs on the Clubhouse terrace overlooking the eighteenth green and only half-conscious of your fluffed shots. More usually the motley crowd that follows professional tournament golf for the pleasure of seeing the occasional three-putt (*see* PUTT).

'Gimme' The conceding of a very short putt to your opponent in MATCH play. The habit of accepting such welcome gifts may not stand the long HANDICAP player in good stead in STROKE play where every SHOT must be played out for the record. He may then find himself short of practice with these putts which have their own special neurotic HAZARDS (*see* 'HABDABS'). The serious player would do well to accept the 'gimme' with gratitude but carry on putting out for practice, having, of course, taken the precaution of clearly establishing in advance that the putt had already been conceded.

'Gobble' (USA) A boldly hit putt which finds the hole (*see* 'LUCK').

Golf   Said to derive from German *kolbe*, French *chole*, Dutch *kolf* or Scottish *gowffe* ('to strike hard'). Must have been played in Scotland earlier than 1457 because in that year the Scottish king James II decreed that 'Futeball and Golfe, or uther sik unproffitable sportis be utterly cryed down and not used', as these games were diverting interest from the more martial art of archery. A subsequent statement by James IV in 1491 on similar lines proves how little notice was taken of the earlier.

Golf widow   A lady whose husband or sweetheart leaves her to her own devices for three or four hours on a Sunday while he plays golf, and who can find nothing useful to do in that time.

Green   Once meant the whole course, e.g. green committee, greenkeeper are concerned with the entire course, rather than just with the magic circle surrounding the flagstick. Now defined as 'all ground which is specially prepared for putting'. 'Fast' or 'slow' greens are so described depending on whether your poorly executed putt shoots past the hole or stops well short. 'Fairly good condition' is the grudging accolade bestowed on the general state of the greens by a player who has just come in with a good MEDAL-round score.

Greenkeeper   The bronzed, muscular factotum responsible for the daily state of the entire course. Usually to be seen motoring round the fairways on a tractor apparently aimlessly, in all weathers, or at rest in his hut scanning the 'Greenkeepers Wanted' column in *Golf Weekly* to check on current pay scales being offered in the trade. Often a man of infinite charm, with an affable manner and a plus-two handicap. Always a good captive audience for a boring shot-by-shot account of your round of golf when it is difficult to detect the glazed expression in his eyes, narrowed to slits by long exposure to the elements.

Greensome   A match in which each side of two partners drives at every hole. The side then chooses which ball it

Greenkeeper

will be advantageous to play and the match then continues as a FOURSOME, striking alternate shots. Players who feel they are deprived of their full quota of drives in a foursome can talk a proposed foursome into a greensome by playing on the natural preference of most golfers for the thrill of having a swipe at the ball on every tee. Said to have been invented by Sir Lycett Green, a well-known Norfolk golfer.

Grip   The way you arrange your hands to hold a club, varying between the overlapping to the interlocking and the two-handed. Whichever you use and are used to, some busybody will encourage you to switch to the other, with dire results.

Gross   Your total score in a MEDAL round. Aptly named.

Ground under repair   is defined in the RULES as 'any portion of the course so marked, and includes material piled for removal, or a hole made by a greenkeeper even if not so marked'. Your ball can be removed from such ground and replaced without PENALTY. In practice, areas marked with a small metal notice 'Ground Under Repair' are permanent bare patches which rarely show any evidence of repairs ever carried out.

'Habdabs' An attack of the screaming (cf. jitters, dreaded lurgies, nadgers, or just plain nerves). A neurotic state of immobility which suddenly seizes a player addressing a putt only inches away from the hole, normally in competition play.

Half 1. A hole is 'halved' (or 'squared') when each side holes out in the same number of STROKES. Similarly a game is halved if neither side is ahead in holes on completing a round. 2. A half pint of bitter at the NINE-TEENTH, but 'I'll have the other half' can mean a half pint of bitter, *or* another large Scotch or gin. *Caveat emptor.*

Handicap An arbitrary figure from nought (SCRATCH) to twenty-four (thirty-six in the case of ladies) allocated to a member by the Club's Handicap Committee, to adjust his score to a common level and indicating his relative ability as a golfer. It is intended to enable the player to return in summer conditions a NETT score off the MEDAL tees equal to the STANDARD SCRATCH SCORE of his Club course. To maintain your current handicap at most Clubs requires the submission of at least two MEDAL score cards per year showing that you have played at least to your handicap figure. Much talk, banter and downright unpleasantness centres on this subject of handicap. Members are considered by others to have a 'phoney' handicap when they manage to win a game, or even a single hole, against a player with a lower handicap, or indeed when they win a Club competition off *any* handicap.

Hazard Defined as any bunker or water hazard. Bare patches (unless marked 'Ground Under Repair'), scrapes, roads, tracks, and paths are not hazards according to the RULES. 'A water hazard is any sea, lake, pond, river, ditch, surface drainage or other open water course, regardless whether or not it contains water, and anything of a similar nature'. In other words, your guess is as good as mine, but generally you add a STROKE to your score if you find your way into an official hazard.

'Head up' The all too common fault of lifting the head during the striking of a ball, resulting in a poor SHOT. Usually followed by an agonized shriek from the player as though stung by a passing wasp.

Hickory North American walnut tree from which club shafts were made before 1929, when the Royal and Ancient permitted the use of steel shafts. Veterans still mourn the passing of the hickory shaft, remembering their halcyon days of golf, if indeed they ever existed. Certainly in the right hands, scores in rounds of golf were as low with hickory shafted clubs as they are now with the use of such new-fangled materials as graphite, laminated plastic and so on.

Hole (cup, USA) 1. The actual metal or plastic pot sunk in the green which is journey's end to all your efforts from the tee. 2. The whole length from tee to pin. The hole is specified to be $4\frac{1}{2}''$ in diameter and at least $4''$ deep. The diameter varies, however, with your performance. A hole suddenly enlarges to the size of a bucket when

Agonized shriek

you are putting well, and shrinks commensurately when you are not. Holes are said to be infested with the 'wee men' when your ball drops and re-emerges as though pushed out by some inside agency. (cf. OUTSIDE AGENCY.)

Inside agency

Hole in one ('ace', USA**)** The miraculous sinking of
a single shot from the tee, required by custom to be
celebrated by drinks all round at the bar. Insurance cover
can be taken out against this eventuality as it could be a
very expensive business, particularly after a Sunday round
at an over-populated golf club. The present writer recently
had a hole in one, but fortunately, with his dog as the only
witness, the event went unrecorded on the Club's honours
board. Total cost of celebration, one large scotch for the
player and a veal bone for the dog. Mr Ted Spong, greenkeeper at the writer's home Club, has been playing golf
with a handicap of four for forty years, without having
scored a single hole in one. His small boy aged ten, out
on his first practice round ever, scored a hole in one with
a 4-wood off a Ladies Tee.

Hole-out   To make the final STROKE of playing the ball into the hole. Optional with your opponent's permission in MATCH play but compulsory in stroke or MEDAL play.

Honour   The side or player winning the previous hole is entitled to play first from the next tee, and is said to have the 'honour'. Sometimes acknowledged with a modest curtsey.

Hook   Opposite fault to a SLICE, the ball fading to the left. Said to be a 'good' fault. A slice for a left-handed player.

Hole-in-one

Identification The act of lifting a ball for the purpose of, except in a HAZARD, when lifting is not allowed. This must be done in the presence of your opponent, and the ball replaced without improving your LIE, or more accurately without *showing* you've improved it.

'Interesting' An understatement to describe any especially difficult hole, or any SHOT your opponent is about to play from a virtually impossible LIE.

Iron Any club from one to ten which is not wooden-headed. 'Any old iron?': a bitter comment made when a wooden-headed player fluffs an iron shot. 'Old iron': description of your set of clubs for the purpose of a trade-in by a pro when he wants to persuade you to flog them for a new set.

'Justice' As in 'There's no justice in this game'. A comment made when a player's ball, in his own judgement well-struck, finds its way into a bunker or runs through the green. Or more to the point, when his opponent's ball, badly struck, finds its way through the same bunker and on to the green. (Cf. 'LUCK'.)

Interesting shot

LGU Ladies Golf Union, organized in 1893 to govern women's golf. Has its own method of handicapping and special provisions under the Royal and Ancient. The first lady golfer is claimed to be Mary, Queen of Scots, who was charged at her trial, prior to being beheaded in 1584, with indifference to the fate of her murdered husband Darnley, in that she played golf a few days after his death. Wives who constantly charge golfer husbands with indifference can be reminded of this royal precedent. (*See* GOLF WIDOW.)

Ladies tee A tee separate from the men's tee, and marked 'LGU'. Has not so far been made an issue of by Women's Lib. Always good for a laugh if used mistakenly by a man.

'Leather mashie' Term applied to a caddie's shoe when it is used surreptitiously to nudge a player's ball on to an improved LIE.

'Legs, no' A putt which pulls up well short of the hole is said disparagingly to have 'No legs'. The anthropomorphic concept of applying human characteristics to an inanimate object, unfairly.

Leather mashie

Expertise

Lesson An hour's session on the practice ground with the pro in which he tries with infinite patience to teach a newcomer the elements of the swing or iron out the golfing problems of a Club member. It comprises the hitting of dozens of practice balls to a monotonous litany of hackneyed but essential instructions. Half the period is taken up retrieving the balls, and the most enjoyable part of a lesson is to watch the pro flick practice balls from the ground into a ball bag with the expertise of a conjurer. Without consulting any timepiece, a pro will contrive to conclude a lesson, pocket the fee, and be back in his shop exactly five minutes before the hour is up.

Level fours (fives) An aid to keeping MEDAL scores. Eighteen holes completed in an average of four STROKES per hole equals a GROSS score of seventy-two. LEVEL FIVES, i.e. ninety gross, is more applicable to the mediocre golfer when he is not at his usual sixes and sevens. Henry Cotton recently expressed his current age as being 'five under fours'.

Lie 1. The way your ball comes to rest on fairway or in rough. It can be 'hanging' or 'downhill' depending on the slope, or just plain impossible. It is useless to try to invite sympathy by saying 'Just look at this awful lie' and expect your partner or opponent to come over and look at it. 2. A word used to ask the current state of the game, *viz.* 'How do you *lie*?' when the minor emphasis seldom goes unmarked.

Like A STROKE which makes a player's score equal to his opponent's on a given hole, as in 'I'm playing the like'.

Links A natural seaside course among sand dunes, but instances abound of links far from the sea. Don't take bets on this definition.

Local knowledge What your host knows about the course he has invited you to play on. Worth several STROKES to him. Also a description of any erratic SHOT your opponent makes which somehow manages to come right in play.

Locker room The changing room in Golf Clubs which seldom has any lockers available. There is some inverted pride about those which offer fewest amenities. Also a place where by tradition doubtful stories are said to be exchanged, but 'you never hear as many these days as you used to'.

Loft To elevate the ball. Also the backward slant on a club face.

Doubtful stories

Long game   Where distance is the more important factor (ant. SHORT GAME) as in 'My long game is good, but my short game is awful', or vice versa.

'Long way to go yet'   A remark made by a player in MATCH play which is meant to comfort an opponent who is so far behind in holes that he hasn't a cat in hell's chance of ever catching up.

Lost ball   A ball is deemed lost if not found within five minutes, give or take ten minutes. (*See* 'DO PLEASE CARRY ON'.)

'Lots of golf left'   A critical comment on a putt which in the opinion of your opponent is just too lengthy to concede. In consequence you ADDRESS the putt nursing a grievance on the meanness of your opponent and with your pride bruised by the implication that you could miss such an elementary putt. The result often is that the putt *is* missed, giving your opponent the opportunity to reiterate his claim that there was 'a lot of golf left' in that putt, in spurious self-justification. (*See* 'NOBBUT A MINUTE'.)

'Luck'   That elusive quality needed in the performance of most games but more especially in golf, judging by the frequency with which it is invoked. Balls which are struck wildly into trees and ricochet safely on to the fairway, flukey chip shots off the green which find their way into the hole, are examples of Luck's bounty. Putts which drop and then pop out of the hole, and straight, long shots on the fairway which kick malevolently into the rough, are examples of bad, or lack of, Luck. A statistical study of a round of golf will prove incontrovertibly that every player has an equal share of both good and bad breaks, but the latter are invariably remembered to the exclusion of the former.

'Make a name for yourself' An encouraging remark
made to the last player in a FOURBALL to drive off at a
short hole when none of the preceding drives have made
the green. Put to such a test, the player so encouraged
rarely rises to the occasion. (*See* 'VIRGIN GREEN'.)

Marker 1. A movable black and white painted post
set in the ground with a metal roundel atop, indicating
the direction of a green unsighted from the tee. Often
hit with bull's-eye precision by players whose direction
of shot anywhere else on the fairway is rarely accurate.
2. A scorer in STROKE play appointed by the committee
to record a competitor's score. 3. A small plastic disc like
a large drawing pin used for marking a ball on the green.
Very difficult to find if kept in the same trouser pocket
as your assortment of tees, but makes its presence felt
sharply if kept in the back pocket when you are sitting
in your car on your way home from golf.

Mashie Until the turn of the century this was the most
lofted club in the bag, equivalent to our No. 5 iron. So
called to describe the mashing effect on a ball if used by
an inexpert player. MASHIE NIBLICK, equivalent to a
No. 7 iron.

Match play   A game played by holes, whereas in

Medal play (or stroke play)   you play in competition against the PAR of the course. Your total or GROSS score minus your HANDICAP figure gives you your medal or NETT score.

Member   A member of a Golf Club can be a full, a five-day, an honorary or an artisan member. All members have a responsibility to adhere to the RULES of golf, etiquette and local rules. In general if you replace your DIVOTS, keep moving on the course, stand your whack in the bar, and pay your sub. promptly, preferably by banker's standing order, you will pass muster. If you are part of one of several small cliques or factions you will claim that the Club is a very matey and sociable one. If you are not a member of any clique or faction you will claim that the Club has too many cliques and factions. Full members feel superior to five-day members who limit their play to weekdays at a reduced annual sub. and can be upstaged at social gatherings by full members who express surprise at never having seen the five-day member on the course. The five-day member can ring the changes by implying that his job is so top level as to allow him to play mid-week golf while preferring to devote his weekends to the family or, if he wishes to ram the point home, to *sailing*.

Mind   'It's all in the mind!' A pseudo-psychological analysis of a player's poor performance given without fee by his partner or opponent, adding an additional problem to what the unfortunate player thought was only a physical one. A corollary is that the most important distance in golf is the four inches between the ears.

Mixed foursomes   A man and woman *v.* a man and woman, with all the traumas to be found in bridge.

'Money player'   Any player who wins a hole against the run of play is described as such, regardless of whether there is a wager on the game or not.

Mulligan   A very unofficial dispensation with any poor first drive, your second counting as your first with no PENALTY incurred. Useful in after-lunch business golf. (*See* 'CLIENT'S GAME'.)

Vital distance

'Nae bother' (Scot.) Description of any average shot that keeps out of trouble. Another case where it may be useful for feigning Scottish ancestry. (cf. 'YOU'RE AWA'.)

Nassau (USA) A form of betting in golf in which a wager is put on the first nine holes, the second nine and the outcome of the match. (For a minor form of Nassau, *see* 'BALL-A-BALL-A-BALL'.)

Nett The total score for a hole or for a round, minus a player's STROKE or HANDICAP. Much jollity can be aroused in the NINETEENTH by playfully confusing GROSS and nett scores. A member's wife who once rang the Clubhouse to explain her husband's absence due to illness said he was running a temperature of 102. 'Gross or nett?' asked a callous bystander. (Author's original story, apocryphal but copyright.)

'Never up, never in' An old golf saw as applied to putting, implying that a ball not putted right to the hole has no chance of ever dropping. This most self-evident of golf truisms is trotted out monotonously when you have putted short, and as an excuse when your putt whistles past the hole.

Niblick   Old fashioned term for a No. 9 iron. Said to be a corruption of Scottish *'neb laigh'*, or broken nose, referring to the short club-face, originally designed for playing out of cart ruts.

'Nineteenth'   The Clubhouse bar. What you repair to after the eighteenth, with or without a brief stop at the locker room.

'Nobbut a minute'   In MATCH play a player faced with a miniscule but perhaps decisive putt, may arch his eyebrows enquiringly at his opponent hoping to have the putt conceded. The latter, ignoring the mute appeal, and using the vernacular to temper the rebuff, may say 'It'll take nobbut a minute' (i.e. 'It won't take a minute to sink it'). Der. hard-headed Yorkshire.

'No idea'   A self-critical judgement made by a player of his own game if playing badly. Never, repeat *never*, made by one player of another's game in the latter's hearing, such is the *esprit de corps* in golf, but 'My partner has *no* idea today' is permissible *sotto voce* by your partner to your opponents.

'Nothing to this game'   A remark, notably lacking in conviction, made by a player who has unexpectedly made a good shot or bogeyed a hole. Rarely repeated during the rest of that particular round.

'Not how, but how many'   A riposte to an opponent who criticizes a poor shot you have just played but which manages to reach the pin, the inference being that it is not the aesthetics that count in golf but the score. (*See* 'COMMERCIAL'.)

'*Nobbut a minute.*'

Obstruction Anything artificial, whether erected, placed or left on the course, with certain exceptions. If movable it may be moved, if immovable, the ball may be moved without PENALTY.

'One!' A tiresome and predictable comment when a player's ball accidentally falls off the tee-peg during the ADDRESS, said half-jocularly in the faint hope that an inexperienced player will actually add a PENALTY STROKE to his score for that hole. Should be treated with contempt. (*See* 'DON'T WANT THAT ONE BACK!' and 'SHOT!')

One-armed bandit 1. Fruit machine now found in most Clubhouses, proceeds from which contribute a substantial income to Golf Clubs. Any machine that does not gush forth a jackpot on inserting your first coin is said to be 'fixed'. 2. Air Chief Marshal Sir 'Gus' Walker, KCB, CBE, DSO, DFC, AFC (Ret'd), whom I can never beat off his eighteen handicap.

'Only a game' A general comment on the game of golf made by a player to comfort an opponent who is having a bad round. Seldom accepted in the spirit in which it is offered.

Open, The Instituted at Prestwick, Scotland by the Prestwick GC in 1860 and taken over by the Royal and Ancient in 1919. A STROKE competition open to professionals and amateurs after qualifying rounds, it is the year's most prestigious event in the golfing calendar, with a similar Open taking place in the USA. From the simple award of a champion belt in 1860 the prizes have now become pretty astronomical.

'Opens up the hole' An encouraging description of an opponent's SHOT which he has managed to play out of the rough to any spot on the fairway vaguely within sight of the green.

Outside agency A human, as distinct from an inanimate OBSTRUCTION. Defined in the Rules as 'any agency not part of the match, or in STROKE play, not part of the competitor's side, and includes a referee, a marker, an observer or a forecaddie'. If a ball at rest is moved by such it may be replaced without PENALTY. If a ball in motion 'lodges in' an outside agency (e.g. in his or her clothing) it may be dropped without penalty. If a ball in motion is accidentally stopped or deflected by an outside agency it must be played as it lies without penalty. No mention is made in the Rules about dragging the prostrate body of the agent struck by a ball out of the way to give the player an unobstructed SHOT.

'How far d'you reckon my ball might have gone, dammit,
if it hadn't struck you on the head?'

PGA Professional Golfers' Association. The pro's trade union (not yet affiliated to the TUC).

Par In theory, perfect play. An arbitrary figure laid down for a hole or for the aggregate score of the eighteen holes, which a SCRATCH player might be expected to take in summer conditions. 'One under par' contrasts strangely with the colloquial and lay use of this phrase. (*See also* BOGEY.)

Partner The chap who plays on your side in a FOUR-BALL, FOURSOME or GREENSOME. (He becomes your 'opponent' in a SINGLES or THREEBALL.) You use his Christian name when the game is going in your favour, and fall back on the impersonal 'Partner' when his bad play loses your side the hole. Thus, 'Oh, *bad* luck, Partner', said with barely concealed venom.

'Pawnbroker' Old fashioned term for a THREEBALL.

Penalty Loss of a STROKE or strokes, or even disqualification, for certain breaches of a RULE of golf. A nasty aspect of the game, especially in MATCH play and

'Oh, bad luck, partner.'

best avoided by making friendly dispensations with your opponent in advance.

Pin   Flagstick.

Pin-high   1. A shot to the green landing level with the pin. 2. How you feel when missing a short putt.

Pitch   An approach SHOT in which the ball is lofted in a high arc. PITCH MARK: an indentation made in the surface of a green by a pitched shot and which should be levelled out by the conscientious golfer.

Pitch-and-run   An approach SHOT in which part of the distance to the pin is covered by the forward roll of the ball after it reaches the ground.

Pivot   The body or lateral hip shift said to be yet another essential element of the golf swing. Reduced to a minimum the older you get.

Plugged   A ball embedding itself in a rain-sodden fairway or green can be claimed to be plugged or 'suckered', and may be lifted without PENALTY. A tetchy opponent will walk quite a long way to inspect a ball declared plugged before agreeing to its being lifted.

Plus-fours   Trousers or knickerbockers strapped at the calf and worn with long woollen socks. At one time what every smart golfer wore.

Plus-two   A HANDICAP rating of *minus* two. (*Sic.*)

Plus-twos   A narrower version of plus-fours, still sported by traditionalists but now looking distinctly old-time beside the flared candy stripes and overcheck creations in vogue at this writing.

Practise   The boring process of swinging at balls on a practice tee, fairway or ground. Recommended by pros and better players ostensibly to improve your game, but really to keep you off the actual course. On competition days, competitors may practise shots before playing but not on the putting green or deliberately towards any of the holes.

Press, pressure, pressing   The act of overhitting or overswinging at the ball with dire results, in inverse ratio to the amount of effort expended. The maxim 'the harder you hit 'em the less distance they'll go' is the most difficult in golf for lesser players to absorb. On the other hand, some of the great natural golfers maintain that their prowess at the game is due simply to 'just going up to the ball and 'itting it 'ard'.

Priority   In the absence of special RULES, SINGLES, THREESOMES or FOURSOMES have precedence over any other kind of MATCH (e.g. THREEBALL or FOUR-BALL). A competition match takes precedence over a friendly match. Any match playing a whole round is entitled to pass a match playing a shorter round. If a match fails to keep its place on the course and loses more than one hole on the players in front, it should allow the match following to pass. Members of golf committees are inclined to get pretty uptight on this matter of priority and it would pay the average Club member to brush up on this particular aspect of etiquette.

Professional   The immaculately dressed chap in charge of the pro's shop and golf tuition to whom everyone from Club president to junior caddie pays obeisance. A demi-god, prone to stomach ulcers.

Provisional ball   A ball played as a substitute for one presumed lost, and incurring two PENALTY STROKES so that you are playing three strokes from the tee. The mediocre player is always reluctant to play a provisional ball for fear of repeating his original performance, thus losing *two* balls and dropping *four* penalty strokes.

Putt   A STROKE made on the green with a putter (putting iron) in the direction of the pin with a view to holing out, ideally in a single SHOT. Hence single-putted, two-putted, three-putted, and even on rare and unmentionable occasions, four-putted.

Rabbit Any long HANDICAP player with a handicap longer than yours.

Rabbit-scratch A shallow scrape made in the fairway by a rabbit of the four-legged kind. The two-legged variety make much deeper scrapes. An excuse for improving your LIE.

'Recovery golf' Description of the performance of a player on a hole which he completes in a single figure when he looked in danger of taking double figures.

Rolling A winter rule (local) whereby a ball on a fairway may be rolled over to avoid unnecessary damage to turf due to close LIES. Of immense help to lesser players who dread the lifting of the rule in early spring. You are meant merely to roll the ball over, but an artful player can roll it surreptitiously a couple of feet nearer the hole.

Rough The uncut or partly cut ('semi' rough) areas on either side of a fairway or around the green. If a ball lies in long grass, rushes, bushes, etc. only so much of it may be touched as is needed to identify it, but its LIE may not be improved. Nor may anything growing be moved, bent or broken in the process. The main advantage the mediocre player gets from being continually in the rough is that statistically he has a good chance of finding other balls lost there. Something like 200,000,000 golf balls are bought each year, so that a fair proportion of those they replace must lie lost in the rough on the world's golf courses.

Round Eighteen holes of golf 'played in their stipulated sequence'. The figure of eighteen was an historical accident. Bruntsfield Links, the oldest golf course in the world, used only to have six holes. On the Isle of May there is still a three-hole golf course. At St Andrews, generations of golfers played nine holes out and the same greens were used for playing, instead presumably of merely walking, home, and this practice resulted in the general acceptance of eighteen holes as the standard figure.

Friendly greeting

Royal and Ancient (R & A)   The Royal and Ancient Golf Club of St Andrews, founded in 1754. The holy of holies, and the governing body of golf. Bow and withdraw backwards. The R & A framed the code of law for the game and gives decisions on disputes which are accepted throughout the world. In 1951 the United States Golfing Association accepted the sovereignty of the R & A.

'Rub of the green'   This is said to occur when a ball in motion is stopped or deflected by an outside agency, i.e. anyone not part of a competitor's side, including a marker, a referee or forecaddie. Used now colloquially to mean *C'est la vie.*

'Rubbish!'   A form of friendly greeting shouted across adjacent fairways by a player in one MATCH to a player in another who has just taken his SHOT, but not intended as a comment on that particular shot.

Rules The Rules of Golf as laid down by the Royal and Ancient are forty-one in number, comprising 25,000 words and 350 special decisions. Few Club golfers are conversant with more than a few essential Rules and even for these interpretations are constantly sought. In addition there are local rules, framed by individual Club Committees covering special circumstances relating to each course.

Ryder Cup Named after Samuel Ryder. A biennial competition between British and American pros, the venue alternating between the USA and Britain. The USA scored their first win in 1934 and have won all but one since. Something to do with superior putting, or the bigger ball, or a bigger population to draw on, or something.

Notifiable disease

Schenectady A putter with a central shaft. One of the early alleged aids to better putting.

Scratch A HANDICAP of nought. Hence SCRATCH MAN, a player who receives no handicap allowance. To retain their cherished zero, scratch men must return cards in at least five competitions per year, their GROSS score equal to or lower than the STANDARD SCRATCH SCORE (q.v.) of the day for the competition concerned, and of these competitions at least two must be on a course other than their home Club. Purely academic information as far as the average Club golfer is concerned.

Sclaff (Scot.) 'A slight blow'. To hit the ground behind the ball, resulting in a fluffed shot.

Secretary The paid official and administrator of a Golf Club. Usually a retired senior army officer supplementing his pension and meant to be as familiar with the Catering Wages Act as with the Rules of Golf. Seldom is.

Shank A short stabbing or socketing shot made by hitting a ball other than with the face of the club-head, sending the ball at an acute and alarming angle to the right. Pros are terrified of shanking, even of discussing the aberration, and consider that it should be a notifiable contagious disease.

Short game   Approach shots and putts. (cf. LONG GAME.)

Shot   American synonym for STROKE, e.g. 'I shot eight-nine this morning'. American Club golfers rarely divulge their official HANDICAP but prefer to say what they 'shoot' in the region of.

Single   A match in which one player plays another. In STROKE play a player playing with another is strictly a COUPLE, there being no such terms in golf as a 'twosome'. A player out on a course alone has no standing and is treated by all and sundry as a displaced person. The same player pairing up with another anywhere on the course immediately re-establishes his legitimacy, but the resulting single must still give way to other matches.

Single-figure   A member of the golfing *élite* with a HANDICAP of one to nine.

Slice   The old banana SHOT, endemic to long HANDICAP players. The agonizing process of trying to cure it is worse than the disease. (*See* BEGINNER'S LOOP.)

Snatch   A convulsive yank of the club from the top of the swing. Part of the anxiety neurosis of long HANDICAP play.

Spoon   A wooden club, originally either long, middle or short, depending on the angle of the face. Now a No. 3 wood.

Square   A match is said to be all square when the score is even. (*See* HALF.)

Stableford   A form of competition played under STROKE conditions against a fixed score at each hole. Named after its inventor, Dr Stableford of Wallasey. HANDICAP strokes to the extent of seven-eighths of your handicap figure, are taken according to the stroke index on the card, and points are awarded varying from one point for a hole done in one over the fixed score to five points for a hole completed in three under the fixed score. Always a more attractive form of competition for the lesser player than a MEDAL, because in a Stableford you can 'blow up' at a hole and perhaps make up for it in points at a succeeding one. Hope, in Stableford, springs eternal.

Stance   The position of the feet at the ADDRESS. 'Square' when the feet are in a line parallel to the ball, 'open' when the left foot is behind the right, 'closed' when the right foot is behind the left. The beginner falls naturally into one or other of these stances but is constantly nagged to change to another for improved performance. Rarely succeeds.

Standard scratch score (SSS)   The aggregate figure in which a SCRATCH player is expected to play round a course from the MEDAL tees in summer conditions. For a normal course of 6,300 yards the SSS is seventy, plus or minus one stroke for every 200 yards variation in length.

Steward   The white-coated gentleman i/c bar, dining room, and general amenities at a Golf Club. An authority on when the bar is closed under social committee rules or when lunch is off. The more amiable are said to be the least efficient and vice versa.

Stick   Flagstick. Also 'Didn't give it enough stick' when a shot falls short of its required length, due to not striking the ball firmly enough or not using the appropriate club.

'Straight at the back of the 'ole, sir'   Advice on the greens by a caddie who has long given up trying to initiate golfers into the BORROWS and other subtleties of putting. More familiar to members of a certain Club in the Home Counties but meriting a wider audience.

Bar closed . . .

Straight left arm   The ideal positioning of the left arm, extended to form a constant radius for the wide arc of the true golf swing. Demonstrated to perfection in photographs or film of most of the young lithe exponents of the professional game. Arguable in the case of the middle-aged golfer.

Stroke   1. Any forward movement of the club 'made with the intention of fairly striking at and moving the ball'. Can be made to look like a mere practice swing by some. 2. A PENALTY added to your score for an infringement of a RULE. 3. Something subtracted from your score on the basis of your handicap at specified holes according to the STROKE INDEX. STROKE PLAY is the more correct version of MEDAL play where the result of a MATCH is determined by strokes rather than holes.

Stroke hole   Hole at which a HANDICAP STROKE is given.

Stymie Not now in use but once a vital element in MATCH play when your opponent's ball on the green is laid in a line between yours and the hole by intention, making it virtually impossible for your ball to be putted to the hole without striking his. Controversy raged for years over this rare ploy in a game of which it is a basic principle that one player's efforts are not directly influenced by his opponent's. Finally in 1951 it was ordained that the stymie be abolished. Since then, the offending ball has to be lifted and marked to allow the opposition an unobstructed putt. Der. Scot. 'styme'; 'Not to see a styme' meaning not to see at all. Or from Dutch '*stuit mij*' (pron. 'stytmy') 'It stops me'.

Suggestion book A dog-eared register found lying around the Clubhouse in which are written suggestions or criticisms varying from the comic-trivial to the serious-helpful. Seldom read by anyone high enough in the Club hierarchy for the suggestions to be implemented.

Sunningdale A friendly arrangement in a SINGLES in which a player who loses two holes in succession receives a STROKE at the next hole. Said to have been invented at Sunningdale G C.

Sweet spot A mythical spot somewhere near the dead centre of a club-face which manufacturers claim will produce the perfect shot if correctly connecting with the ball. Vague enough to evade the Trade Descriptions Act.

Swing The co-ordinated series of motions starting with the ADDRESS and ending with the follow through. Space, fortunately, forbids going into detail of the many and varied elements which comprise the golf swing.

Tee 1. A platform of ground from which a player drives his ball towards the hole. Provided with golf furniture ranging from two simple markers numbering the hole, to wooden seats, ball cleaners on stands, rubber mats for winter play, depending on how posh the Club is. The tee markers are changed around to avoid wear on the tee, and the type of tee is indicated by the colour of the marker, e.g. red for mid-week play, yellow for TIGER or competition play, and white for LGU. 2. The wooden or plastic peg on which the ball is placed for a drive, superseding the historic pinches of sand from the now defunct sand box.

Tee off, up To place a ball on a tee peg on the teeing ground preparatory to driving off. At the start of a game precedence is decided by the toss of a coin, thereafter by whichever side or player has the honour (q.v.).

Temporary greens are substitute greens prepared on the fairway near the actual greens when the weather is so severe, e.g. snow, ice, that their surface needs protection. Most greenkeepers take special delight in recommending the closure of the entire course on any weather pretext.

Failing that, they will insist on temporary greens even though this must give them extra work in their preparation. Circular sections in the fairway have to be mown to simulate a green and holes and flags inserted, but the surface is seldom suitable for serious putting. A round of golf on temporary greens is played for the exercise rather than for enjoyment.

Texas Wedge A putter, used in unorthodox fashion to play a ball from the fairway to the green and towards the hole, is elevated in status to the mythical Texas Wedge, as though it were some new mysterious addition to your set of clubs.

Through the green Official description of 'the whole area of the course except the teeing ground and putting green of the hole being played, and all the HAZARDS on the course'. To the average golfer 'through the green' simply means his ball running across the green into the rough beyond.

Tiger A short HANDICAP player, as opposed to that other, but minor, zoological specimen, the RABBIT (q.v.).

Timing Yet another of the essential ingredients in the successful striking of the ball. Having got your stance and grip right, your swing must be timed correctly. This timing always seems to be elusively between a swing that is too fast and one that is too slow. Hence the constantly re-iterated 'My timing's right off today'.

Topping The act of striking the ball on the head instead of in the middle, or 'meat', where it does most good, and sending it scuffling ignominiously a few yards ahead.

Topspin A motion imparted to a ball which sends it past the pin if misapplied or up to the hole if correctly struck.

'Trouble!' Description of any badly hit ball on its way into deep rough.

Wrong ball

Under-clubbing A drive which falls short of reaching the green at a short hole can be blamed on not using a big enough club, or more likely not hitting with the big enough club correctly.

Unplayable A ball is said to be unplayable when a player himself deems it so, and it may be declared unplayable anywhere on the course. The ball may be lifted and replaced within two clubs' length of the original spot but not nearer the hole, with a PENALTY of one STROKE. One of the few occasions in golf when a player can be his own judge and jury.

Up In MATCH play a side is up when it has won more holes than it has lost. (cf. DOWN.)

'Virgin green' A green on a short PAR-three hole which players in a THREE- or FOURBALL have all failed to reach with their drive. (*See* 'MAKE A NAME FOR YOURSELF'.)

'Visible'   A polite description of a SHOT which although a poor one has not run into trouble.

Walker Cup   Named after George H. Walker, President of the US Golf Association in 1920, it is a biennial international competition for British and American top amateurs, the venue, like the Ryder Cup, alternating between the USA and Britain. Since 1922 the USA has won all except one by huge margins.

Wedge   An open-faced club used for short pitches around the green (pitching-wedge) or in bunkers (sand-wedge). The request 'Pass me a sand-wedge' runs the risk of the witty riposte 'The ham or the cheese?'

'Whenever I get a card in my hand...'   A despairing comment made by a player in a STROKE competition blaming his poor play on the anxiety induced by playing under competition conditions. Actually it is never his own card that he marks but his opponent's.

'Worker', a   An indifferent SHOT which contrives to keep going, usually along the ground in the direction of the green.

Wrong ball   In MATCH play a player who plays the wrong ball except in a HAZARD loses the hole. In a hazard he is excused provided he then plays his own ball. When players mistakenly exchange balls, the first to play the wrong ball loses the hole. In STROKE play, the PENALTY is two strokes. It is always wise practice to announce the make and number of your ball to your opponent before driving off, if only to ensure that you are not both playing the identical type. One of the saddest stories in golf is of two women players on a Surrey course who neglected to compare balls on the tee of a short hole. Both hit the green with their drives and on reaching the hole discovered that one of them had holed-in-one, but neither could claim it as such because both were playing a Dunlop 65–5.

Zaharias, Mrs Mildred 'Babe' Famed American woman golfer who won the British Women's Amateur Open in 1946. Also the 1954 US Women's Open Championship with a prodigious score of 291 for four rounds. She is included here not only to record her prowess, but to conclude an A–Z glossary with a Z.